ALPHA & OMEGA

Living Secure Between The Beginning and the End

Gerard Assey

ALPHA & OMEGA:
Living Secure Between The Beginning and the End

By

Gerard Assey

Published by:
Gerard Assey
19/18, Palli Arasan Street
Anna Nagar East
Chennai - 600 102

ISBN: 978-81-998781-5-0

Table of Contents

PREFACE

There are books that are written from study. There are books that are written from observation. And then there are books that are written from walking through something you did not choose—but could not escape.

This book: **"ALPHA & OMEGA: *Living Secure Between the Beginning and the End*"** was born in the middle.

Not at the beginning of a dream. Not at the triumphant end of a testimony. But in the in-between space where faith is no longer theoretical and trust is no longer poetic. It was shaped in conversations with people who love God deeply yet quietly ask, *"Why does the middle feel so unstable?"*

Most believers have no trouble celebrating God as Creator. We rejoice in the language of Genesis. We declare that He is Alpha. We also cling to the promise that He will complete what He began. We sing about eternity. We hold onto heaven. We proclaim that He is Omega.

But what about the long stretch between those two declarations?

What about the years of waiting?

The seasons of silence?

The prayers that seem delayed?

The detours that make no immediate sense?

It is in that middle space that many faithful people wrestle—not with whether God exists, but with whether He is involved. Not with whether He is powerful, but with whether He is present.

This book is not an attempt to explain every mystery. It is an invitation to see the middle differently.

The revelation that God is Alpha and Omega is not meant to decorate theology; it is meant to stabilize life. If He truly stands at the beginning and the end, then nothing in between is outside His authorship, authority, or awareness. The middle is not accidental. It is intentional. It is not abandonment. It is development.

Throughout these pages, you will encounter biblical lives that were shaped in their in-between seasons—Joseph in prison before the palace, David in caves before the crown, Abraham walking toward promises he could not yet see fulfilled, the disciples locked in rooms before they were sent into nations. Their stories are not ancient relics; they are mirrors.

You will also meet ordinary people—business owners, mothers, professionals, men and women navigating loss, accusation, delay, and redirection. Their names may be unfamiliar, but their struggles are not. Their journeys remind us that the theology of Alpha and Omega must be lived in boardrooms, kitchens, hospital rooms, and quiet prayer corners.

This book does not promise quick fixes. It does not offer formulas to eliminate tension. Instead, it offers perspective.

- ✓ *If you are in a season where God feels silent, this book is for you.*
- ✓ *If you are navigating uncertainty about your calling, this book is for you.*
- ✓ *If you are weary from waiting, this book is for you.*
- ✓ *If you have ever wondered why the middle feels harder than the beginning, this book is for you.*

My prayer is simple: that as you turn these pages, you will begin to see your story through heaven's lens. That you will discover that maturity is formed in the middle. That you will find courage to trust the Author even when you cannot see the final chapter.

You are not forgotten in your process.

You are not overlooked in your delay.

You are not lost in your detour.

The One who began your story is faithful.

The One who will finish it is sovereign.

And between those two eternal declarations, you are held—secure, seen, and steadily being shaped.

Welcome to the middle!

INTRODUCTION
Living in the Middle

There are two parts of the Christian story that most believers embrace without much resistance. We celebrate the beginning, and we long for the end.

We rejoice that God is Creator. We find comfort that He formed the heavens and the earth, as declared in the opening words of the Book of Genesis. We sing with confidence that He is coming again, as promised in the closing visions of the Book of Revelation. We love the idea of God as the First and the Last, the Alpha and the Omega.

But what unsettles us is not the beginning. And it is not the end.

It is the middle.

It is the season between promise and fulfillment.

Between prayer and answer.

Between calling and clarity.

Between crisis and closure.

Most believers do not struggle with the theology of Alpha and Omega. They struggle with the experience of living between the two.

When the Lord declares in Isaiah 44:6, *"I am the First and I am the Last; besides Me there is no God,"* this is not poetic flourish. It is prophetic assurance. It is not a decorative description of God's nature. It is a stabilizing revelation meant to anchor anxious hearts. In Revelation 1:8, He announces, *"I am the Alpha and the Omega… the Almighty."* And again in Revelation 22:13, *"I am the Alpha and the Omega, the Beginning and the End, the First and the Last."* These are not lyrical repetitions. They are covenant declarations.

He is not merely present at the beginning and waiting at the end.
He occupies both simultaneously.
The One who stands at your starting point is the same One who is already present at your conclusion.
Yet we live in the space in between. And that space can feel frightening.

The Danger of Middle Anxiety

Middle anxiety is the quiet torment of uncertainty. It is the fear that what has started may not finish well. It is the suspicion that God may initiate something but somehow allow it to collapse halfway.
We see this anxiety in the wilderness wanderings of Israel. God delivered them powerfully from Egypt in the Book of Exodus. The Red Sea parted. Pharaoh's army was defeated. The beginning was dramatic and undeniable. But in the middle — in the desert — they panicked. They questioned whether the God who began their deliverance would bring them into the Promised Land.
Their fear was not about Egypt anymore. It was about the in-between.
In Numbers 14, they spoke of returning to bondage because the journey seemed too uncertain. They believed in the Alpha who rescued them from slavery. They struggled to trust the Omega who would establish them in promise.
Middle anxiety makes us forget past miracles and doubt future faithfulness.
We also see this tension in the New Testament. In the Gospel of Mark 4, when a storm erupted on the Sea of Galilee, the disciples woke Jesus in panic and asked, *"Teacher, do You not care that we are perishing?"* The One who had called them to cross

over to the other side was in the boat with them. Yet in the middle of the storm, they doubted His commitment to complete what He had initiated.
The storm did not mean absence. It revealed anxiety.
How often have we done the same? We celebrate salvation. We anticipate heaven. But when the marriage feels strained, when finances tighten, when diagnosis reports arrive, when doors close unexpectedly, we whisper the same question: *"Lord, do You care?"*
Middle anxiety is the silent erosion of trust.

The Illusion of Control

Another reason the middle unsettles us is because it exposes how little control we actually possess.
Beginnings feel manageable. We plan them. We prepare for them. We launch new ventures, ministries, relationships, and seasons with excitement and strategy.
Endings, at least in our imagination, feel defined. We picture victory, restoration, completion.
But the middle refuses to obey our timelines. It disrupts our systems. It humbles our confidence.
In the Book of Job, Job's life shifts from abundance to devastation in a matter of chapters. He loses wealth, children, health, and reputation. The beginning of his story presents him as righteous and blessed. The end reveals restoration and deeper revelation. But the middle—those long speeches, those silent nights, those misunderstood conversations—tests everything he believes about God.
Job's suffering exposes the illusion that righteousness guarantees predictable outcomes. The middle strips away the myth of control.

In the New Testament, consider Peter. In the Gospel of Luke 5, he leaves everything to follow Jesus. That is a decisive beginning. In the book of Acts, he stands boldly at Pentecost, preaching with power. That is a triumphant outcome. But between calling and courage lies denial. In Luke 22, he fails publicly and bitterly weeps.

Peter's middle includes shame.

The illusion of control says, *"If I start well, I will finish well without interruption."* The reality of sovereignty says, "God finishes well, even when the middle exposes your weakness."

Alpha and Omega means that God's purposes are not fragile. They do not depend on our flawless performance.

Alpha & Omega: Prophetic Assurance, Not Poetry

When God declares Himself the First and the Last in Isaiah 48:12, He speaks to a people who are about to enter exile. They are facing displacement and humiliation. In that context, His self-revelation becomes deeply personal. He is saying, in effect, *"Empires may shift. Kings may rise and fall. But I remain. And because I remain, your story is not over."*

Alpha and Omega is not abstract theology. It is covenant language.

It means that before you were born, God already stood at the horizon of your life. It means that your last chapter is not written by circumstance but by sovereignty.

This revelation stabilizes faith. It steadies families. It anchors callings. It guards destiny.

When a believer truly understands that God is both origin and outcome, comparison loses power. Fear loses voice. Desperation softens into trust.
You stop living as if every interruption is a catastrophe. You begin living as if every interruption is included.

Daniel Varghese: A Life in the Middle
Daniel Varghese had always believed in God. He grew up in church, memorized Scripture, and could quote Genesis 1:1 with confidence. He believed God created the world. He believed in eternal life. He believed Jesus would return one day.
But he did not know how to trust God when everything collapsed between those two certainties.
Daniel built a mid-sized logistics company over fifteen years. It was not overnight success; it was slow, disciplined growth. He often testified that God had blessed the work of his hands. He gave generously. He prayed before major decisions. From all outward appearances, his beginning was marked by faith.
Then came the collapse.
A global supply chain disruption combined with a major client defaulting on payments triggered a financial spiral. Within six months, Daniel's company went from stable to insolvent. Loans were called in. Assets were liquidated. Employees he had known for years lost their jobs. Overnight, he went from respected entrepreneur to cautionary tale.
The hardest part was not the financial loss. It was the silence.
He prayed, but heaven felt quiet. He attended church, but worship felt distant. He believed God had created him with purpose. He believed God promised

eternal life. But in the middle, between past blessing and future hope, he felt abandoned.

One evening, sitting alone in his dimly lit office before handing over the keys, Daniel opened his Bible to Revelation and read: *"I am the Alpha and the Omega… the Almighty."*

For the first time, those words confronted him.

If God was Alpha, then God had been present at the beginning of his business.

If God was Omega, then God was already present at whatever came next.

The collapse had not surprised God. The bankruptcy filing had not disqualified Daniel's calling. The middle was not evidence of divine neglect.

That realization did not instantly restore his finances. But it restored something deeper: perspective.

Over the following months, Daniel began mentoring young entrepreneurs who were just starting out. His experience, once a source of shame, became wisdom for others. Two years later, he launched a smaller, leaner consultancy built on lessons learned in failure.

Looking back, he would say, *"I knew God as Creator. I knew Him as the One who prepares heaven. But I did not know Him as the God of the in-between. The day I understood that He was already standing at my ending, my fear lost its authority."*

Daniel's story frames this book because it mirrors so many of ours. We trust God at the altar of beginnings. We sing about Him at the promise of endings. But we wrestle in the corridor between.

Living Secure in the Middle

To live securely between the beginning and the end is not to deny difficulty. It is to redefine it.

It is to see wilderness as transition, not abandonment.

It is to see storms as passage, not destruction.

It is to see delay as development, not denial.

When believers grasp that God is Alpha and Omega, they stop measuring their lives by temporary turbulence. They begin measuring by eternal authorship.

The middle may be messy. It may include questions, tears, unexpected detours, and humbling lessons. But it is not random.

The same God who declared light into darkness in Genesis stands sovereign over the closing pages of Revelation. And that same God governs the pages you are currently living.

You are not suspended in uncertainty.

You are held between certainty.

This book is an invitation to trust the God who writes beginnings and completes endings. It is a call to release the illusion of control and embrace the comfort of sovereignty. It is an awakening to the reality that the One who stands at Alpha is already waiting at Omega.

And if that is true, then the middle — however uncomfortable — is not unsafe.

It is under authorship.

CHAPTER 1
A for AUTHOR
God Writes What He Starts

The Bible does not begin with an argument. It begins with authorship.

"In the beginning God created the heavens and the earth" (Genesis 1:1).

The opening line of the Book of Genesis does not explain God. It reveals Him. Before there was matter, motion, light, or language, there was a Writer. Creation itself is presented as composition. God speaks, and reality responds. Light appears on command. Seas gather into place. Life emerges in layers of intentional order.

Nothing in Genesis 1 feels accidental. The rhythm of the chapter carries structure, progression, and purpose. Evening and morning. Separation and formation. Blessing and multiplication. The world did not stumble into existence. It was written into being.

If that is how Scripture introduces God, then it is how we must understand Him. He is not merely Creator in the mechanical sense. He is Author in the intentional sense.

An author does not create randomly. He writes with end in view.

This is why Isaiah 46:10 declares that God is the One *"declaring the end from the beginning, and from ancient times things that are not yet done."* The Author does not discover the ending; He determines it. He does not guess how the story concludes; He ordains its conclusion before the first sentence unfolds.

If God writes what He starts, then the central question for the believer becomes deeply personal: Is my life under authorship?

The Author Who Writes Beyond Human Betrayal

Few Old Testament narratives display divine authorship more clearly than the life of Joseph in the Book of Genesis.

Joseph's story begins with a dream. A young man sees sheaves bowing and stars aligning. It is a beginning filled with promise. But within a few chapters, the story appears to unravel. He is betrayed by his brothers, thrown into a pit, sold into slavery, falsely accused, and imprisoned.

If Joseph's life were reduced to the middle chapters, it would read like tragedy. Betrayal by family. Exploitation by strangers. Injustice by authority.

Yet the Author never abandoned the manuscript.

The pit was not a deletion. It was a paragraph.

The prison was not the ending. It was a transition.

Years later, when Joseph stands as governor of Egypt, positioned to preserve nations during famine, he speaks words that reveal profound theological insight: *"You meant evil against me; but God meant it for good"* (Genesis 50:20).

Joseph does not deny the evil. He does not minimize the pain. But he recognizes authorship. The same event carried two intentions—human malice and divine purpose. One intended destruction. The other intended deliverance.

Only an Author can take betrayal and weave it into preservation.

When you read Joseph's life backward, you see coherence. But when he lived it forward, he saw confusion. The Author knew the palace was coming while Joseph was still in chains.

If God is Author, then your pain has placement. It is not random ink spilled across your story. It sits where it sits because it serves something larger than the moment.

The Author Who Restores Failed Characters

The New Testament gives us another portrait of divine authorship in the life of Peter.

Peter's calling begins with boldness. He leaves his nets at the invitation of Jesus. He walks on water, confesses Christ, and declares loyalty. But in Luke 22, under pressure and fear, he denies Jesus three times. The rooster crows. The disciple who once declared unwavering faith weeps bitterly.

If Peter were editing his own life, that scene would never have made it into the book.

Failure feels like the end of authorship. It feels like the page has been torn out and thrown away.

But the story continues.

In the Gospel of John 21, after the resurrection, Jesus meets Peter by the sea. There is no public humiliation, no rejection. Instead, there is breakfast and restoration. Three times Jesus asks, *"Do you love Me?"*—mirroring the three denials. Then He commissions Peter: *"Feed My sheep."*

The Author does not discard the character because of one flawed chapter.

Peter's denial did not cancel his destiny. It became part of his shaping. The man who would later preach boldly at Pentecost was the same man who had tasted personal weakness. That weakness did not disqualify him; it deepened him.

If God is Author, then your failure does not surprise Him. He writes restoration into the narrative long before you realize you need it.

Your delay has design. Your detour has direction.

Anita Rao: When Rejection Preserves Destiny

Anita Rao believed she had reached the happiest chapter of her life. She was engaged to a man she had known for two years. The families had met. Plans were underway. Invitations were drafted.

Then, abruptly, everything collapsed.

Her fiancé confessed he was not ready for marriage and withdrew from the engagement. There was no dramatic scandal, no clear betrayal—just retreat. Anita felt exposed and humiliated. Friends whispered. Relatives speculated. She replayed conversations endlessly, searching for what she had done wrong.

For months, she prayed with confusion. She had asked God to bless the relationship. She had felt peace. Now she felt abandoned. She wondered whether she had misheard God or whether God had mismanaged her life.

The middle felt unbearable.

Over the next year, Anita reluctantly accepted a temporary overseas assignment through her company. It was not part of her original plan, but staying in her hometown felt suffocating. In that new environment, she met colleagues from diverse backgrounds, rediscovered her confidence, and began serving in a small local church.

There she encountered a different rhythm of faith—quieter, deeper, less performative. She met Daniel, a widower with a young daughter. Their friendship developed slowly, rooted not in excitement but in maturity. Over time, she came to see that her earlier relationship, though promising, had lacked emotional depth and shared spiritual direction.

Years later, reflecting on that painful season, Anita said, *"What felt like rejection was preservation. If that engagement had proceeded, I would have been stepping into something misaligned. I thought God had erased a chapter. Now I see He was editing."*

The abandoned engagement had placement. The delay had design. The detour had direction.

She could not see it while crying on her bedroom floor. But the Author was not absent in that moment. He was composing.

The Deep Revelation of Divine Authorship

When believers truly grasp that God is Author, several truths begin to reshape the way they interpret life.

First, pain is not meaningless. It may not be fully explained, but it is never purposeless. Just as shadows in a painting add depth rather than diminish beauty, difficult seasons often prepare capacity that comfort never could.

Second, delay is not denial. Authors develop characters before they reveal conclusions. A hurried narrative produces shallow transformation. God's timing is not accidental pacing; it is intentional formation.

Third, detours are not mistakes. Sometimes the road you did not plan becomes the path that reveals who you truly are.

Isaiah 46:10 reminds us that God declares the end from the beginning. That means your present confusion does not threaten His future intention. He is not improvising your destiny. He is unfolding it.

The challenge is that we often try to seize the pen. We rewrite conversations in our minds. We attempt to fast-forward seasons. We demand clarity beyond what is given. But premature editing often distorts the narrative.
There is a humility required in living under authorship.

Learning to Trust the Draft
Trusting God as Author does not mean passivity. It means cooperation without control.
There are moments when the healthiest spiritual act is restraint—to stop rewriting chapters God is still drafting. Sometimes we sabotage growth because we cannot tolerate unfinished sentences.
One practical discipline that strengthens trust is journaling unfinished chapters. When you write honestly about what feels unresolved—career uncertainty, relational tension, unanswered prayer—you externalize your anxiety. You place it on paper instead of carrying it solely in your heart. Over time, reviewing those entries becomes evidence of divine continuity. You begin to see how previous uncertainties evolved into testimonies.
Another spiritual posture is learning to pray smaller prayers.
Instead of demanding, *"Lord, show me the whole plan,"* begin to pray, *"Lord, show me the next paragraph."* Authors rarely reveal entire manuscripts at once. They reveal scenes as needed.

God's authorship does not eliminate mystery. It redeems it.
You may not understand why the pit came before the palace. You may not understand why denial

preceded commissioning. You may not understand why rejection preceded alignment. But if He is Author, then coherence exists—even when clarity does not.

Genesis begins with a God who speaks order into chaos. Revelation ends with a God who restores all things. Between those two declarations lies your story.

And if He writes what He starts, then you are not abandoned mid-sentence.

You are still being written.

CHAPTER 2
A for ANCIENT OF DAYS
The God Who Was Before Your Crisis

Every crisis has a timestamp.
There is always a moment when the phone call comes, the email arrives, the report is opened, the door closes, the words are spoken. We remember those moments because they divide life into "before" and "after." Something shifts, and suddenly time feels hostile. The future looks uncertain, and the present feels fragile.
But Scripture introduces us to a God who is not confined to timestamps.
In Daniel 7, the prophet is given a vision of kingdoms rising like beasts from the sea—violent, intimidating, dominant. Empires parade across the stage of history with arrogance and power. Yet above and beyond them, Daniel sees another scene: *"I watched till thrones were put in place, and the Ancient of Days was seated... His throne was a fiery flame... the court was seated, and the books were opened."*
The title "Ancient of Days" is not about age as we understand it. It is about eternality. It is about a God who precedes every empire and outlasts every ruler. Before Babylon flexed its strength, He was. Before Persia organized its armies, He was. Before Rome built its roads, He was. The beasts rise and fall. The Ancient of Days remains seated.
Psalm 90 echoes the same revelation: *"Before the mountains were brought forth, or ever You had formed the earth and the world, even from*

everlasting to everlasting, You are God." The mountains, which feel immovable to us, are described as having a beginning. God does not.

Time does not threaten Him. It serves Him.

That truth changes how we interpret crisis. Because if God was before the mountain, He will be after it. If He was before the diagnosis, He will be beyond it.

Daniel in the Shadow of Empires

Daniel himself lived in turbulent times. He was taken from Jerusalem into Babylonian exile as a young man. His homeland was invaded, his culture dismantled, his future disrupted. The stability he once knew vanished overnight.

Imagine being Daniel—far from home, under foreign authority, watching kings rule with unchecked pride. Nebuchadnezzar builds statues to himself. Belshazzar desecrates sacred vessels. Political tides shift violently. Each regime feels permanent while it stands.

Yet Daniel's visions in the Book of Daniel reveal something deeper than politics. Behind the drama of human power is a throne that never shakes.

Empires are temporary chapters. The Ancient of Days is the eternal Author.

When Nebuchadnezzar is humbled and confesses that God's dominion is everlasting (Daniel 4:34), it is not merely personal repentance. It is a revelation: no ruler outruns the Ancient of Days.

Daniel's security did not come from the stability of his environment. It came from the eternality of his God.

Many believers struggle because they anchor themselves to systems that shift—economies, governments, organizations, even relationships. When those systems tremble, they tremble with them. But Daniel anchored himself to a throne older than Babylon.

If the Ancient of Days was before your crisis, then your crisis is not ultimate.

Jesus in the Storm

The New Testament presents this same truth embodied in Christ.

In the Gospel of Mark 4, Jesus tells His disciples, *"Let us cross over to the other side."* The instruction is clear. The destination is declared. But on the journey, a great windstorm arises. Waves beat into the boat. Water fills the vessel. The experienced fishermen panic.

Meanwhile, Jesus sleeps.

It is one of the most striking contrasts in Scripture. Chaos outside. Calm inside. The disciples cry out, *"Teacher, do You not care that we are perishing?"*

They measure reality by the storm. Jesus measures it by sovereignty.

When He rises and rebukes the wind and the sea, saying, *"Peace, be still,"* the elements obey. The storm that terrified seasoned fishermen submits instantly to His voice.

Why? Because the One in the boat existed before the sea was formed. The One who slept during the storm spoke the waters into existence in Genesis. The waves were not strangers to Him. They were servants.

Time and turbulence do not intimidate the Ancient of Days.

The disciples' fear was rooted in immediacy. Jesus' authority was rooted in eternality.

We panic because we think the storm is larger than our timeline. God remains steady because He stands outside it.

Ravi Menon: When Time Feels Like an Enemy

Ravi Menon was forty-two when the headaches began. They were subtle at first—brief, manageable, dismissible. He blamed stress. He worked long hours, managed a growing business, and balanced family responsibilities. A checkup seemed unnecessary.

But the headaches intensified. One afternoon, while driving home, his vision blurred for a few seconds. That frightened him enough to schedule tests.

The diagnosis came quickly and without gentleness. A rare neurological condition. Progressive. Unpredictable.

Ravi felt as if someone had pressed pause on his future. Words like *"progression," "management,"* and *"uncertain prognosis"* echoed in his mind. He went home in silence. That night, he lay awake staring at the ceiling, asking questions that felt heavier than his body.

- ✓ *How long do I have?*
- ✓ *What will happen to my family?*
- ✓ *Why now?*

Time suddenly felt like an enemy. Every ticking second carried threat. He replayed his past decisions, searching for causes. He imagined worst-case scenarios, projecting fear into years he had not yet lived.

In those early weeks, Ravi's prayers were frantic. He demanded explanations. He bargained. He pleaded.

One evening, his father visited and brought an old Bible Ravi had received as a teenager. It fell open to

Psalm 90. *"Lord, You have been our dwelling place in all generations... from everlasting to everlasting, You are God."*
The words were familiar but distant—until they weren't.
For the first time since the diagnosis, Ravi considered a different perspective. If God was "from everlasting," then God was already present in every tomorrow Ravi feared. If the Ancient of Days stood beyond time, then Ravi's future was not a dark corridor. It was territory already inhabited by God.
The illness did not disappear. The prognosis did not magically reverse. But something shifted inside him. He stopped asking, *"How much time do I have?"* and began asking, *"How do I live faithfully in the time I have?"*
He started attending a small prayer group regularly. He spoke openly with his children about faith and fragility. He reorganized his business so it did not depend entirely on his daily presence. He sought medical treatment responsibly but refused to surrender his peace.
Months later, he would say, *"I thought my life was shrinking. I realized it was being redefined. God was in my tomorrows before I arrived there."*
Time did not threaten God. It served Him.

Time Serves the Ancient of Days
One of the deepest revelations of this chapter is this: God does not move anxiously through time. He governs it.
For us, time feels linear and irreversible. We cannot return to yesterday. We cannot visit tomorrow. We live confined within moments.

But Scripture consistently presents God as sovereign over seasons. Ecclesiastes speaks of a time to plant and a time to uproot, a time to weep and a time to laugh. Those seasons are not chaotic accidents. They are ordered within divine wisdom.

When believers forget that God is the Ancient of Days, they reduce Him to a reactive deity—responding to events as they occur. But Daniel 7 shows us a throne already established before beasts emerge. Psalm 90 reminds us that mountains themselves had a beginning. Mark 4 reveals a Christ who commands nature because He precedes it.

Your crisis may be new to you. It is not new to Him.

Developing Long-View Faith

Learning to live under the revelation of the Ancient of Days requires intentional spiritual formation.

First, panic questions must be replaced with eternal declarations. Instead of asking, *"What if everything collapses?"* begin declaring, *"The One who holds eternity holds me."* Instead of asking, *"How will I survive this?"* begin affirming, *"My times are in His hands."* The questions may arise naturally, but they must not be allowed to dominate your thinking.

Second, study God's faithfulness in history. Scripture is not merely inspirational; it is evidential. When you read how He sustained Israel in exile, preserved Joseph in prison, restored Peter after failure, and strengthened Paul in persecution, you are not reading ancient stories. You are studying patterns. The Ancient of Days has a track record.

History becomes fuel for hope.

Finally, cultivate long-view faith. Short-view faith demands immediate resolution. Long-view faith trusts that what feels delayed may still be perfectly timed.

Daniel waited decades to see certain visions unfold. The disciples endured the cross before they understood resurrection. Ravi Menon learned to measure life not by length alone but by faithfulness.

Long-view faith is not denial of pain. It is refusal to let pain define the entire narrative.

When you know that God was before your crisis and will remain after it, urgency softens into trust. You stop demanding immediate explanations. You begin resting in eternal presence.

The Ancient of Days is not hurried. He is not surprised. He is not scrambling.

He is seated.

And because He is seated, you do not have to live as if everything depends on your panic.

Your crisis has a date. Your God does not.

CHAPTER 3
A for ALMIGHTY
When Power Belongs to the Beginning and the End

There are seasons in life when faith does not fail because God is absent, but because circumstances look stronger than His promises. We do not doubt that God began our story. We even believe He will conclude it well. But in the middle, when pressure mounts and opposition stands tall, we quietly ask, *"Is He powerful enough for this?"*

This is why the revelation of God as Almighty is not optional for the believer — it is foundational.

In Revelation 1:8, the Lord declares, *"I am the Alpha and the Omega… the Almighty."* The statement is not poetic decoration. It is a declaration of dominion. The One who begins is not weak. The One who ends is not uncertain. The same voice that speaks the first word also has authority over the final outcome.

To call God Alpha and Omega without calling Him Almighty would reduce Him to a well-meaning planner without power. But Scripture refuses that notion. The Alpha is Almighty. The Omega is Almighty. Therefore, every chapter in between is under Almighty authority.

If the Alpha is Almighty, then nothing begins outside His capacity. If the Omega is Almighty, then nothing can prevent His conclusion.

Power belongs to the Beginning and the End.

Moses Before Pharaoh: When Almighty Confronts the Impossible

In the book of Exodus, Moses stands before Pharaoh, the most powerful ruler of his time. Egypt was not merely a nation; it was an empire fortified by wealth, military might, and spiritual arrogance. Pharaoh was considered divine. To oppose him was unthinkable.

Yet God sends a shepherd with a staff.

When Moses hesitates, God responds not by changing Pharaoh but by revealing Himself. *"I AM WHO I AM"* (Exodus 3:14). It is a revelation of eternal, self-existent power. God does not introduce Himself as a tribal deity hoping for cooperation. He reveals Himself as the uncreated One who simply is.

Each plague that follows is not random judgment; it is a dismantling of Egypt's false gods. The Nile turns to blood. Darkness covers the land. The firstborn falls. Each act announces the same truth: Almighty power does not negotiate with counterfeit authority.

Moses' confidence did not come from his eloquence. It came from who sent him. The staff in his hand became powerful only because it represented the Almighty.

Here is the deep revelation: Pharaoh was not Moses' real problem. Power confrontation was happening in the unseen realm. When the Almighty stepped into the narrative, the strongest empire of its time could not resist.

If the Alpha is Almighty, the Omega is unstoppable.

The God who initiated Israel's deliverance was powerful enough to complete it — through the Red Sea, through the wilderness, into promise.

Resurrection Power: The Omega Cannot Be Sealed

Centuries later, in the Gospel of Matthew 28, the Roman Empire believes it has finished a problem. Jesus has been crucified. The stone is sealed. Guards are posted. Authority believes it has secured the end of the story.

But heaven had already written the final line.

The resurrection is not merely a miracle. It is a declaration that the Omega cannot be sealed by human systems. The grave had a stone, but the stone had no authority. Death had a moment, but it had no permanence.

When the angel rolls the stone away, it is not to let Jesus out — it is to let humanity see that Almighty power has already acted.

The same voice that said "Let there be light" in the beginning now speaks life into a borrowed tomb. Beginning power becomes ending victory.

The cross looked final. It was not. The tomb looked secure. It was not. The empire looked dominant. It was not.

Almighty means no force, visible or invisible, can overrule the One who stands at both ends of time.

If the Alpha spoke creation into existence, the Omega can speak resurrection out of devastation.

The Almighty in the Middle of Generational Cycles

Grace Fernandes grew up in a family that knew hard work but never knew financial stability. Her grandfather had lost land due to poor decisions. Her father struggled under debt his entire life. Loans were inherited like heirlooms. Conversations around the dinner table were filled with anxiety.

Grace loved God. She believed in salvation. But she quietly believed something else too — that certain cycles were simply stronger than prayer.

When her small tailoring business began, she carried invisible fear. *"What if I fail like the others?"* When unexpected expenses arose, she panicked. *"This is how it begins,"* she would think. *"The pattern is repeating."*

One evening, during a Bible study on Revelation 1:8, the phrase *"the Almighty"* pierced her heart. She had believed God was Savior. She had believed He was loving. But she had never deeply embraced Him as Almighty over systems, history, and inherited patterns.

She began to pray differently. Not emotionally, but authoritatively. *"Lord, if You are Almighty, then debt is not almighty. History is not almighty. My surname is not almighty. You are."*

She started studying financial stewardship. She sought wise counsel. She restructured her business. She cut unnecessary expenses. She created a repayment plan. She honored God with her first income instead of her leftovers.

The cycle did not break overnight. But something shifted internally before it shifted externally. She stopped seeing herself as a victim of legacy and began seeing herself as a participant in divine authority.

Within five years, her business stabilized. Within seven, she was debt-free. Within ten, she was teaching financial literacy in her church.

What changed? Not just income. Revelation.

Grace realized that generational cycles may be strong, but they are not sovereign. Only God is sovereign. Only God is Almighty.

When Power Belongs to the Beginning and the End

We often think our greatest enemy is the size of the opposition. But our real struggle is misjudging power. Pharaoh looked powerful. Rome looked powerful. The grave looked powerful. Debt cycles look powerful. Addiction looks powerful. Fear looks powerful.

But power is not determined by appearance. Power is determined by authority.

The revelation of Almighty God reorders our perspective. It does not deny that Pharaoh exists. It declares that Pharaoh is temporary. It does not deny that tombs exist. It declares that tombs cannot contain eternal purpose.

When God identifies Himself as Almighty in Revelation 1:8, He is speaking to a persecuted church. Believers were facing imprisonment, martyrdom, and exile. To them, Rome seemed unstoppable.

Yet heaven's message was clear: The One who began history will conclude it. And He is Almighty.

Your "Pharaoh" may not wear a crown. It may be fear. It may be a medical diagnosis. It may be a broken relationship. It may be internal insecurity. But none of these are Alpha. None of these are Omega.

And none of these are Almighty.

Identifying Your Pharaoh

Before deliverance can occur, confrontation must be acknowledged. Moses had to stand before Pharaoh. He could not pretend Egypt was harmless.

In the same way, believers must honestly identify what intimidates them. What feels immovable? What narrative has convinced you that change is impossible?

Is it a mindset? A pattern? A dependency? A financial system? A toxic relationship? An internal belief that you are not capable?
When you name your Pharaoh, you position yourself for God to reveal His supremacy.

Daily Supremacy Declarations
Power encounters are sustained by confession. Moses repeatedly declared what God had said. Jesus repeatedly spoke what the Father had promised.
Words align perspective.
Grace began each morning saying aloud, *"God is Almighty over my finances."* It sounded simple, almost repetitive. But repetition reshaped her faith.
Declare daily that God is supreme over your situation. Not as ritual, but as alignment. The Almighty does not need reminding — we do.
Faith-Filled and Practical Steps
Almighty power does not eliminate responsibility. It empowers obedience.
Moses had to lift the staff. The disciples had to go to the tomb. Grace had to restructure her finances. Resurrection power does not replace participation; it strengthens it.
Sometimes believers wait passively for miracles while ignoring wisdom. The Almighty works through instruction as much as intervention.
If the Alpha is Almighty, then the Omega will not fail. But the middle often requires courageous steps.

The Unstoppable Omega
The resurrection of Jesus in Matthew 28 is the ultimate proof that endings belong to God. What

humanity seals, God can unseal. What systems pronounce dead, God can resurrect.
This is why believers can endure the middle.
Because power does not belong to Pharaoh.
Power does not belong to Rome.
Power does not belong to generational history.
Power does not belong to fear.
Power belongs to the One who stands at the beginning and the end.
And if He is Almighty at the beginning, He will be unstoppable at the conclusion.
The question is not whether your challenge is real.
The question is whether it is greater than the Almighty.
And Scripture answers clearly: it is not.

CHAPTER 4
A for ANCHOR
Stability in the Middle

There is something unsettling about the middle of a storm. The beginning of a storm often carries warning. The end carries relief. But the middle feels endless. The sky is dark, the winds are loud, and direction is lost. It is in this middle space that faith is tested most deeply.

The writer of Hebrews speaks into that tension with profound clarity: *"We have this hope as an anchor for the soul, firm and secure"* (Hebrews 6:19). Notice that the anchor is not for the boat. It is for the soul. Boats may still sway. Winds may still blow. Waves may still crash. But the soul can remain steady.

If God is Alpha and Omega, then He is not only the One who starts and finishes; He is the Anchor who holds us steady in between.

An anchor is unseen once it is dropped. It sinks beneath the surface, gripping something solid that the eye cannot see. In the same way, hope in Christ does not always remove visible turbulence, but it connects us to invisible certainty.

The storms of life do not ask for decorations. They expose foundations.

Noah: Anchored Before the Rain Fell

Long before the first drop of rain struck the earth, Noah was anchoring his life in obedience. Genesis 6–8 tells the story of a man who built an ark in obedience to a word from God, despite never having

seen a flood. Genesis 6:22 simply says, *"Noah did everything just as God commanded him."*
The ark was not merely a vessel of survival; it was a physical manifestation of anchored faith.
When the rain began and the fountains of the deep burst open, the world panicked. But Noah did not scramble for direction. He had already received it. He had anchored his future in obedience long before the storm arrived.
It is significant that the ark had no steering wheel. Once inside, Noah could not control direction. The vessel was carried by waters beyond human strength. That is the revelation: when God is your Anchor, you surrender control of the currents.
The flood did not mean God had lost control. The flood was part of His sovereign plan. Genesis 8:1 says, *"But God remembered Noah."* The storm had an appointed end. The waters rose by God's permission and receded by God's command.
If Christ is your Anchor, the storm has boundaries.

Paul: Anchored in the Midst of Chaos
Centuries later, another storm raged—this time in the Mediterranean Sea. Acts 27 describes Paul's voyage to Rome. The ship was caught in a violent storm called the northeaster. The crew lost hope. They threw cargo overboard. For many days, Scripture says, *"neither sun nor stars appeared, and the storm continued raging. We finally gave up all hope of being saved"* (Acts 27:20).
Notice the language: they gave up hope.
But Paul did not.
In the darkest part of the storm, Paul stood and declared, *"Keep up your courage, because not one of you will be lost; only the ship will be destroyed"*

(Acts 27:22). He had received a word from the Lord. While sailors relied on ropes and anchors dropped into the sea, Paul relied on a promise anchored in heaven.

The physical ship would break apart, but the people would survive.

There is a powerful distinction here. God does not always preserve the vessel you traveled in. Sometimes careers break. Sometimes plans collapse. Sometimes structures sink. But when you are anchored in Christ, your life will not be destroyed by what falls apart around you.

Paul's peace did not calm the storm. It calmed the men.

Storms test whether Christ is your decoration or your foundation. A decorative faith looks beautiful in calm weather. An anchored faith holds when visibility is gone.

When Christ Is Decoration

Some believers treat faith as an addition to life rather than the core of it. Church attendance becomes routine. Worship becomes background. Scripture becomes occasional. Christ becomes admired—but not relied upon.

In calm seasons, decorative faith feels sufficient. But storms expose superficial foundations.

Jesus warned of this in Matthew 7 when He spoke of the house built on sand and the house built on rock. The storm was the same. The difference was the foundation.

When Christ is merely admired, anxiety reigns in crisis. When Christ is the Anchor, peace can coexist with turbulence.

Meera Thomas: Betrayal in the Middle

Meera Thomas believed she had a stable family life. She and her husband had built a small but growing business together. They served faithfully in their local church. Life seemed secure.

Then she discovered financial decisions had been made without her knowledge. Funds had been mismanaged. Trust was broken—not only in business, but in marriage.

Betrayal has a unique sting. It is not an external storm; it is a fracture from within.

For months, Meera oscillated between anger and despair. Her prayers felt mechanical. Worship felt forced. The future felt uncertain. She found herself asking, "*Where is God in this?"*

One evening, during a small prayer gathering, a simple verse was read aloud: *"We have this hope as an anchor for the soul."* The words pierced her heart. She realized something profound—she had anchored her peace in her husband's reliability, her business stability, and her predictable routines. When those shifted, her sense of safety collapsed.

But Christ had not shifted.

Slowly, Meera began rebuilding her inner life. She set aside time daily not to solve problems, but to sit in worship. She began journaling Scriptures instead of rehearsing arguments. She sought counsel from mature believers instead of isolating herself. She refused to make permanent decisions in temporary pain.

The external situation did not change overnight. But something within her stabilized.

Months later, reconciliation began—not perfectly, but sincerely. Financial recovery was gradual. Trust was rebuilt step by step. But the greatest transformation

had already happened: Meera's anchor was no longer in outcomes. It was in Christ.
Storms often reveal misplaced anchors.

Emotional Anchoring Through Worship

Worship is not escapism; it is recalibration. When we worship, we remind our soul who governs the storm. David modeled this in the Psalms repeatedly: he would begin with distress and end with declaration.
Worship shifts focus from wind to Word.
When emotions are unstable, worship creates alignment. It tells anxiety that God is still enthroned. It tells fear that eternity is larger than this moment.
Anchored believers do not deny emotion. They direct it.

Anchoring Relationships

Isolation intensifies storms. Even Paul had companions in the ship. Noah had his family in the ark. God often stabilizes us through covenant relationships.
An anchored life is not independent; it is interconnected.
When you choose wise counsel over silent pride, you drop another anchor. When you confess weakness instead of pretending strength, you secure stability.
The church is not merely a gathering; it is a harbor.

Anchoring in Promises, Not Outcomes

Perhaps the deepest revelation in this chapter is this: anchors attach to promises, not predictions.
Outcomes fluctuate. Timelines shift. Human plans change. But the promises of God remain.
Noah did not know when the rain would stop, but he knew God had spoken. Paul did not know how the

shipwreck would unfold, but he knew the angel had assured him of survival.

When God is Alpha and Omega, He governs the beginning and the end of your storm. Your role is not to control the waves but to remain connected to His Word.

Hebrews says this hope is “firm and secure.” The language implies something immovable. Not rigid, but rooted.

You may still feel the wind. You may still experience uncertainty. But beneath the surface, your soul can grip something eternal.

The Revelation of the Anchor

An anchor does not prevent movement; it prevents drift. That is the key.

Without Christ as Anchor, storms cause drift—drift in belief, drift in character, drift in commitment. Small compromises begin. Doubts grow louder. Spiritual disciplines weaken.

But when Christ is your Anchor, storms deepen you instead of displacing you.

The Alpha who began your story has not abandoned you in the middle. The Omega who will finish your story has already secured your destination. Between those two eternal points stands Christ—steady, sovereign, and sufficient.

The question is not whether storms will come.

The question is: what holds you when they do?

CHAPTER 5
A for ARCHITECT
God Designs the End Before the Beginning

Every building begins twice—first in the mind of the architect, and only later in brick and stone. Before foundations are dug, before scaffolding rises, before noise fills the site, there is a design. Lines are drawn. Measurements are calculated. The end is envisioned long before the first visible step is taken.

This is how God works.

In Isaiah 48:12, the Lord declares, *"I am He; I am the First and I am the Last."* This is not merely a statement about His eternity. It is a revelation about His design. He stands at the beginning and at the completion simultaneously. He is not reacting to events as they unfold; He is orchestrating them according to a purpose that precedes them.

If God is Alpha and Omega, then He is also Architect. The blueprint of your life existed in His heart before you existed in history.

We often live as if God is improvising. We pray as if He is surprised. We panic as if He is adjusting. But the revelation of the Architect silences that anxiety. The One who called you into being has already designed your becoming.

The Blueprint Precedes the Building

When Jerusalem lay in ruins, its walls broken and its gates burned, the destruction was visible. What was not visible was the design in God's heart for restoration.

Nehemiah, serving as cupbearer to the king of Persia, heard the report of Jerusalem's condition and wept (Nehemiah 1:3–4). The city of his fathers was vulnerable and disgraced. To human eyes, the story looked finished.

But the Architect had already drawn new plans.

Nehemiah did not rush blindly into action. He fasted and prayed. He sought permission. He surveyed the walls quietly at night before speaking publicly (Nehemiah 2:12–15). Why? Because builders must understand the blueprint before laying stones.

The remarkable thing is that opposition arose immediately. Sanballat and Tobiah mocked and resisted (Nehemiah 4:1–3). The work was threatened by discouragement and fear. Yet Nehemiah declared, *"The God of heaven will give us success"* (Nehemiah 2:20).

The walls were rebuilt in fifty-two days (Nehemiah 6:15). What had been rubble became security again. What looked like permanent ruin became testimony.

Here is the deeper revelation: the destruction of Jerusalem did not cancel God's design for Jerusalem. The blueprint preceded the breakdown.

In your life, what appears to be ruin may simply be renovation.

God's Workmanship

The New Testament echoes this truth with even greater clarity. Ephesians 2:10 says, *"For we are His workmanship, created in Christ Jesus for good works, which God prepared beforehand that we should walk in them."*

The word "workmanship" suggests craftsmanship. It implies intention, artistry, deliberation. You are not an accident of circumstance. You are not a random

collection of experiences. You are a crafted life with prepared works.
Notice the phrase "prepared beforehand." Before you faced that opportunity, it was prepared. Before you encountered that trial, grace was assigned. Before you discovered your gifts, they were designed.

The Architect does not build aimlessly.
Sometimes we treat our lives like construction sites where chaos reigns. We see scaffolding, dust, delay, and assume disorder. But construction often looks messy before it looks magnificent.
God's work in you may feel unfinished, but unfinished does not mean unplanned.

Arjun Patel: When Plans Collapse
Arjun Patel had always been driven. From university onward, his goal was clear: climb the corporate ladder, secure financial stability, and provide for his family in a way his parents never experienced.
He excelled. Promotions came steadily. Recognition followed. Then, without warning, a company restructuring eliminated his position. Years of effort evaporated in a single meeting.
Arjun was stunned. He felt embarrassed, angry, and confused. Had he misheard God? Had he failed? Was this punishment?
For weeks, he oscillated between frantic job applications and silent frustration. The blueprint he had drawn for his life was crumpled.
One evening, while reading Isaiah 48:12, he paused at the words, *"I am the First and I am the Last."* A quiet realization formed: if God stands at both ends of his story, then this termination was not outside divine awareness.

Slowly, Arjun began to pray differently. Instead of asking, "Why did this happen?" he began asking, "What are You building through this?"

In the months that followed, he accepted a temporary consulting role with a nonprofit organization. It paid less but exposed him to community development work. He discovered a passion for mentoring young entrepreneurs from underprivileged backgrounds.

What he once saw as a setback became a rerouting.

Years later, Arjun would look back and admit that losing his corporate role was the doorway into his calling. The Architect had not abandoned him; He had redirected him.

The blueprint was larger than the salary.

Seeking the Blueprint, Not the Applause

Nehemiah did not rebuild the wall for applause. In fact, much of the work was resisted and criticized. Yet he remained focused on the assignment.

One of the greatest distractions in the middle of construction is the desire for approval. Applause tempts us to modify the blueprint to suit public opinion.

But the Architect designs according to purpose, not popularity.

When believers anchor their identity in human validation, they begin altering divine design. They choose visible success over eternal significance. They build additions God never drew.

If God is Architect, our task is not to impress the crowd but to interpret His plan.

This requires prayerful listening. It requires patience. It requires humility to admit that we may not yet see the full design.

What Is God Constructing Through This?

Every challenge carries constructive potential. Nehemiah's opposition strengthened unity among the builders. They worked with a tool in one hand and a weapon in the other (Nehemiah 4:17). Adversity clarified purpose.

Likewise, Ephesians reminds us that we are being formed for good works. Trials often chisel character. Delays develop endurance. Closed doors redirect ambition.

When something painful unfolds, instead of assuming demolition, consider construction.

Ask what God is shaping in your character. Ask what dependency He is deepening. Ask what hidden strength He is forming.

The Architect sees the finished structure. You see scaffolding.

Pruning or Punishment?

One of the most important discernments in the middle of change is understanding the difference between pruning and punishment.

Punishment is retribution for rebellion. Pruning is refinement for fruitfulness.

In John 15, Jesus explains that the Father prunes fruitful branches so they may bear more fruit. Pruning involves cutting—but not to destroy. It removes excess so life can flow more effectively.

Arjun initially interpreted his job loss as punishment. But over time, he recognized it as pruning. His identity had become entangled with position. God removed the excess so calling could emerge.

Nehemiah faced ridicule, but it was not punishment. It was resistance against divine progress.

When circumstances shift, ask: Is God correcting sin, or is He cultivating strength? The answer shapes your response.

The Architect's Patience

God does not rush construction. Foundations take time. Reinforcement is often invisible. Strength is embedded before beauty is displayed.

You may feel delayed. But delay is not denial. It may be reinforcement.

Isaiah's declaration that God is First and Last assures us that the Architect does not abandon projects midway. He does not run out of resources. He does not forget His design.

He finishes what He begins.

If He designed your purpose before your birth, He will not misplace it in your middle.

Living Under Design

To live under the revelation of God as Architect is to walk with quiet confidence. It does not eliminate struggle. It does eliminate chaos.

You may not know every detail of the blueprint, but you trust the Designer. You may not understand every season, but you believe in divine intention.

Nehemiah rebuilt walls stone by stone. The church in Ephesus grew believer by believer. Arjun rebuilt his vision step by step.

Construction is incremental. Revelation is progressive. But the design is eternal.

The Alpha who initiated your existence has already envisioned your Omega. Between those two divine declarations, He is constructing something beautiful—sometimes through success, sometimes through loss, always through purpose.

The blueprint precedes the building.
And the Architect never makes mistakes.

CHAPTER 6
A for ADJUDICATOR
God Has the Final Word

There are moments in life when it feels as though the verdict has already been delivered. A diagnosis is spoken. An accusation is made. A door is shut. A reputation is questioned. And in those moments, the human heart trembles because it assumes that what has just been declared is final.

But Revelation 1:17 records a powerful scene. John, overwhelmed by the vision of the glorified Christ, falls at His feet *"as though dead."* Then Jesus lays His right hand on him and says, *"Do not be afraid. I am the First and the Last."*

In other words, I speak first—and I speak last.

This is not simply a statement about chronology. It is a declaration of authority. The One who is Alpha and Omega is also the Adjudicator. He renders the ultimate decision. Human voices may rise, circumstances may pronounce their judgments, and even time may appear to settle matters—but none of these have the final word.

God does.

The revelation that God is Adjudicator steadies the soul in seasons of misunderstanding, delay, and apparent defeat. It reminds us that premature conclusions are often wrong conclusions.

Job: When Heaven Speaks After Silence

Few stories in Scripture illustrate this more painfully than the life of Job. In a single devastating sequence, Job loses his wealth, his children, and his health.

What had been stability becomes ash and sorrow. His friends arrive, and instead of comfort, they offer accusations disguised as theology. They assume his suffering must be punishment.

For chapter after chapter in the Book of Job, there is debate, confusion, and anguish. Job cries out. His friends reason poorly. Silence from heaven feels heavy.

But silence is not absence.

When the Lord finally speaks in Job 38, it is not with explanation but with revelation. God asks, *"Where were you when I laid the earth's foundation?"* The point is not to shame Job but to reestablish perspective. The Creator of galaxies is not scrambling to manage one man's suffering. His wisdom transcends human interpretation.

In the end, Job 42:10 tells us that the Lord restored his fortunes and gave him twice as much as he had before. The same friends who accused him were corrected by God.

The verdict of heaven overturned the verdict of assumption.

What looked like divine abandonment was actually divine confidence. God had trusted Job's faith to endure testing.

Here is the deeper revelation: the long middle of silence does not cancel the certainty of God's final word. Delay is not denial when Omega speaks last.

Lazarus: When Death Seems Final

In John 11, another situation appears irreversible. Lazarus falls ill. His sisters, Mary and Martha, send word to Jesus. They believe He can heal. Yet Jesus does something that confounds them—He delays.

Scripture says plainly, "So when he heard that Lazarus was sick, he stayed where he was two more days" (John 11:6). It is one of the most mysterious verses in the Gospel. He loved them, yet He waited.

By the time Jesus arrives, Lazarus has been in the tomb four days. Martha meets Him with both faith and disappointment: *"Lord, if you had been here, my brother would not have died"* (John 11:21).

To human reasoning, the verdict was sealed. Death had spoken.

But Jesus responds with a revelation: *"I am the resurrection and the life"* (John 11:25). He does not merely promise resurrection; He embodies it. Then He stands before the tomb and calls, "Lazarus, come out!" (John 11:43).

And death releases its hold.

The delay had a purpose. Jesus says earlier in the chapter that this sickness would not end in death but would reveal the glory of God (John 11:4). What appeared final was simply the stage upon which God would demonstrate authority.

When Alpha and Omega stands at the grave, the grave does not get the last word.

Samuel D'Souza: Living Under Suspicion

Samuel D'Souza had built his career carefully over fifteen years in a multinational firm. He was known for diligence and integrity. Then a financial discrepancy surfaced in his department. An internal review began. Quiet whispers circulated.

Though the investigation was ongoing, suspicion landed heavily on him. Meetings felt tense. Conversations grew shorter. Friends at work became cautious. His name, once associated with reliability, was now attached to doubt.

Samuel was devastated. He replayed conversations in his mind. He imagined worst-case outcomes. At home, his anxiety spilled into silence. He wanted to defend himself publicly, to confront colleagues, to expose inconsistencies.

But a trusted mentor reminded him gently, "Let God be your Adjudicator. Don't rush to defend what He can vindicate."

It was not easy. Weeks stretched into months. The investigation felt like an endless hallway with no doors. Samuel resisted the temptation to lash out or resign impulsively. Instead, he continued performing his duties faithfully. He guarded his words carefully, refusing to criticize leadership or speculate about others.

In quiet prayer, he often repeated Revelation 1:17: "I am the First and the Last." If Christ is the Last, then no human report is ultimate.

Eventually, the truth surfaced. The discrepancy was traced to an external vendor's error. Samuel was formally cleared. In a surprising turn, leadership commended him for his composure during the process.

But the greater victory was internal. He had learned to wait for God's verdict.

Vindication is sweeter when it comes from heaven.

Refusing Premature Conclusions

One of the enemy's sharpest tools is the whisper of finality. *"It's over." "You've failed." "This is permanent."* These conclusions often form long before God has spoken.

Job's friends concluded he was guilty. Martha concluded it was too late. Samuel concluded his career was ruined.

Premature conclusions rob faith of endurance.
When we rush to interpret circumstances without consulting eternity, we imprison ourselves within limited perspective. The Adjudicator sees the full record. He weighs motives, contexts, and hidden factors. His judgment is neither hasty nor incomplete.
Learning to resist premature conclusions requires humility. It means admitting that what appears obvious may not be ultimate.

Guarding the Tongue in the Middle

Storm seasons tempt us to speak from pain rather than wisdom. Words spoken in frustration can outlive the trial that birthed them.
Job, despite his anguish, refused to curse God. He wrestled, questioned, lamented—but he did not renounce. Samuel resisted gossip. Martha, though disappointed, still declared faith: “But I know that even now God will give you whatever you ask” (John 11:22).
Guarding the tongue in seasons of accusation or delay protects future restoration. It keeps bitterness from hardening into identity.
The Adjudicator does not need our emotional outbursts to defend us. He requires our trust.

Waiting for the Verdict

Waiting is not passive. It is active trust. It is choosing obedience while the case is still open. It is believing that silence does not equal abandonment.
Job’s restoration did not erase his suffering, but it reframed it. Lazarus’ resurrection did not undo the grief of those four days, but it revealed a greater glory. Samuel’s clearance did not erase the

discomfort of suspicion, but it strengthened his character.
The common thread is this: God's verdict arrived after human verdicts had been spoken.

Delay is not denial when Omega speaks last.
The One who declares Himself the First and the Last is reminding us that history begins in His voice and concludes in His authority. Your reputation, your calling, your future—none of these are ultimately determined by human opinion.
When accusations rise, when diagnoses threaten, when circumstances pronounce defeat, remember this: heaven's court is still in session.
And the Adjudicator has not yet spoken His final word.
If you belong to Him, that word will not be defeat.
It will be redemption.

CHAPTER 7
A for ALL-IN-ALL
Nothing Exists Outside Him

There is a subtle danger in the way many believers live. We affirm that God is the Beginning. We celebrate that He is the End. But in the quiet routines of ordinary life, we behave as though the middle belongs to us.

We compartmentalize Him.

He is Lord of Sunday, but consultant on Monday. He is invited into crisis, but not necessarily into conversation. We worship Him in church, but strategize without Him in business. We thank Him for blessings, but rarely recognize Him in interruptions.

Yet Scripture presents a far greater vision.

In Colossians 1:16–17, Paul writes of Christ, *"For in Him all things were created: things in heaven and on earth, visible and invisible… all things have been created through Him and for Him. He is before all things, and in Him all things hold together."* A few verses later he adds that Christ is to have "the supremacy" in everything (Colossians 1:18).

Not in some things. In everything.

If He is Alpha and Omega, then He is also the substance of every letter in between. Nothing exists outside Him. Nothing holds together without Him. Nothing finds meaning apart from Him.

The revelation of God as All-in-All dismantles the sacred-secular divide and invites us to live consciously within His presence in every sphere.

Abraham: Walking With God Through Every Season

Abraham's journey from Genesis 12 to 22 is not a series of isolated spiritual moments; it is a life woven together with God in every decision.

In Genesis 12, God calls Abram to leave his country and go to a land He would show him. The promise is grand: a great nation, a great name, blessing to the families of the earth. Abram obeys, not knowing the full map.

But the story does not move in a straight line of triumph. There are famines. There are detours into Egypt. There are moments of fear when Abraham misrepresents Sarah as his sister. There are long years of waiting for a promised son. There is the painful complexity of Hagar and Ishmael. There is laughter in the birth of Isaac. And finally, there is the unimaginable command in Genesis 22 to offer Isaac on Mount Moriah.

Through it all, one thing remains consistent: Abraham builds altars.

He builds an altar when he arrives in Canaan (Genesis 12:7). He builds another between Bethel and Ai (Genesis 12:8). The altar becomes a symbol that God is not confined to one event but integrated into the entire journey.

God is present in promise and in famine. In laughter and in testing. In delay and in fulfillment.

By the time Abraham stands on Mount Moriah, ready to surrender Isaac, he has learned something profound: God is not merely the giver of blessings; He is the center of life itself. When the ram appears in the thicket, Abraham names the place *"The Lord Will Provide"* (Genesis 22:14).

Provision was not just about a sacrifice. It was about revelation. Abraham had discovered that God was not confined to moments of miracle. He was All-in-All.

Paul: Christ as Life Itself

Centuries later, Paul writes from prison in Philippians 1. His circumstances are restrictive. His future is uncertain. Yet his words are astonishing: *"For to me, to live is Christ and to die is gain"* (Philippians 1:21).

Notice the structure of that statement. Paul does not say, *"Christ is part of my life."* He says, *"To live is Christ."* Christ is not an addition to existence; He is its definition.

In Colossians, Paul declares that all things hold together in Christ. In Philippians, he lives as though that is true.

Prison cannot remove Christ from his calling. Opposition cannot silence Christ's purpose. Even death cannot threaten his hope. Why? Because Christ is not merely at the beginning of Paul's salvation story and at the end of his eternal destiny. Christ fills the entire space between.

When Paul preaches, works, suffers, rejoices, plans, or waits, it is all Christ.

This is the revelation of All-in-All: faith is not an activity we perform. It is an atmosphere we inhabit.

Leah George: Discovering God in Every Compartment

Leah George once believed that God moved most powerfully in church services and conferences. She loved worship nights and retreats. But everyday life felt ordinary—sometimes exhausting.

She was a mother of two young children, managing a small home-based baking business. Her days were filled with school runs, invoices, laundry, deadlines, and the unpredictable emotions of toddlers. Occasionally she would feel guilty, as though she was drifting spiritually because she did not have hours for extended prayer.

Then a season of loss changed her perspective. Leah's mother passed away after a brief illness. Grief entered her home quietly but deeply. In the midst of mourning, she still had to pack lunchboxes and respond to customer messages. Life did not pause.

One afternoon, while reading Colossians 1, she was struck by the phrase: *"In Him all things hold together."* All things. Not only sermons. Not only ministry platforms. All things.

She began to see that motherhood was not separate from spirituality. Business decisions were not outside God's presence. Grief was not beyond His companionship. Joy was not independent of His goodness.

Instead of dividing her life into sacred and secular, she started inviting God consciously into each task. While kneading dough, she prayed for the families who would eat her bread. While folding clothes, she thanked God for the lives those clothes represented. While grieving her mother, she spoke honestly to God about her pain instead of suppressing it.

Gradually, the awareness of God became less event-based and more constant.

She realized something transformative: God was not waiting for her in a special place at a special time. He was present in the kitchen, in the classroom, in the hospital room, in the marketplace.

Nothing existed outside Him.

Integrating Faith Into Every Compartment

The revelation that Christ is All-in-All dismantles the illusion that some areas of life are spiritually neutral.

Work becomes worship when done in dependence on Him. Parenting becomes discipleship when shaped by His wisdom. Grief becomes sacred ground when processed in His presence. Success becomes stewardship when surrendered to His glory.

Abraham did not only meet God at dramatic moments; he walked with Him across decades. Paul did not confine Christ to synagogue sermons; he carried Him into prison cells and shipwrecks.

Integration requires intention. It means asking, in ordinary decisions, “Lord, how do You see this?” It means acknowledging Him not only in crisis but in routine. It means recognizing that the same God who governs eternity also cares about invoices, homework, conversations, and private thoughts.

When Christ is All-in-All, spirituality ceases to be seasonal.

Removing the Sacred-Secular Divide

One of the quiet distortions in modern faith is the idea that ministry is sacred and marketplace is secular. That prayer is sacred but spreadsheets are not. That preaching matters more to God than parenting.

But Colossians corrects this fragmentation. If all things were created through Him and for Him, then every legitimate vocation becomes a context for glorifying Him.

Abraham’s calling involved herds and land negotiations. Paul made tents. Leah baked bread.

None of these were distractions from God's purpose; they were arenas in which His purpose unfolded.

When believers live divided lives, they experience divided devotion. But when they recognize that nothing exists outside Christ's authority and presence, every moment becomes an opportunity for communion.

Living Consciously Within God

To live consciously within God is not mystical detachment from reality. It is heightened awareness of reality's true source.

It means beginning the day acknowledging that you exist in Him. It means pausing before major decisions and inviting His wisdom. It means recognizing His hand not only in miracles but in maintenance. It means understanding that joy is not accidental and sorrow is not unnoticed.

Abraham discovered that God was present in promise and in test. Paul discovered that Christ was present in life and in death. Leah discovered that God was present in motherhood, business, loss, and laughter.

If He is Alpha and Omega, then He fills the entire span of your existence. There is no neutral ground. There is no corner of life where He is absent.

When this revelation settles into the heart, anxiety decreases. You are not navigating isolated compartments alone. You are living, moving, and having your being in Him.

Christ is not an accessory to your story.

He is the atmosphere of it.

And when you begin to see that nothing exists outside Him, every moment—ordinary or extraordinary—becomes sacred ground.

FINAL CHAPTER
Don't Fear the Middle

Every meaningful story has a middle.

The beginning introduces promise. The end reveals fulfillment. But the middle carries tension, conflict, uncertainty, and development. It is in the middle that characters are formed. It is in the middle that motives are tested. It is in the middle that faith either deepens or dissolves.

Many believers love the language of Genesis and Revelation. We celebrate that God is the Creator. We rejoice that Christ is returning. We proclaim that He is Alpha and Omega. Yet most of our lived experience is not in the beginning or the end. It is in the in-between.

And the middle can feel long.

There are seasons when prayers seem unanswered, when progress appears invisible, when promises feel delayed. It is here—far from the excitement of new beginnings and far from the clarity of final outcomes—that maturity is forged.

The middle is not a mistake in your story. It is the making of it.

Middle Seasons Define Maturity

Consider the life of David. When the prophet Samuel anointed him in 1 Samuel 16, it was a sacred interruption to an ordinary day. Oil flowed over the head of a shepherd boy. Destiny was declared. Scripture says the Spirit of the Lord came powerfully upon him from that day forward.

It looked like the beginning of something immediate.

But between the anointing and the throne stretched years of obscurity and adversity. David served Saul faithfully, soothing his torment with worship. Yet the same king he served eventually hunted him like prey. David hid in caves. He wandered through wilderness terrain. He tasted betrayal and rejection.

The promise was undeniable. The process was unbearable.

And yet, the middle made the king.

In the cave of En Gedi, when David had the opportunity to kill Saul and claim the throne prematurely, he restrained himself (1 Samuel 24). That restraint did not come from ambition; it came from maturity. The wilderness had carved patience into him. The caves had formed character that the palace would require.

God was not absent in David's delay. He was refining him.

In the New Testament, the disciples experienced a similar middle. When Jesus called them, they followed Him with expectation. They saw miracles, heard the Sermon on the Mount, watched thousands fed with a few loaves. They believed they were moving toward visible triumph.

Then came the cross.

The arrest shattered their confidence. The trial exposed their fear. The crucifixion dismantled their assumptions. Between Good Friday and Resurrection Sunday, heaven seemed silent. Doors were locked. Hope appeared buried.

That dark middle transformed them.

When the risen Christ appeared, their faith was no longer dependent on spectacle. It was anchored in resurrection. The same men who scattered in fear would later stand boldly in Jerusalem declaring the gospel in the book of Acts.

Maturity does not grow in comfort. It grows in process.

God Finishes What He Authors

Scripture quietly but consistently assures us that God does not abandon His work halfway.

Ecclesiastes 3:11 declares that He makes everything beautiful in its time. Philippians 1:6 reinforces it: *"He who began a good work in you will carry it on to completion until the day of Christ Jesus."*

The Author does not leave chapters unfinished.

Joseph's life in Genesis is one of the clearest demonstrations of this truth. He received dreams of prominence as a young man. But soon after, he was betrayed by his brothers, sold into slavery, falsely accused, and imprisoned.

His middle was long and unjust.

Yet Genesis 39 repeats a quiet refrain: *"The Lord was with Joseph."* Not only in Potiphar's house. Not only when he interpreted dreams. Even in prison.

When Joseph finally rose to power in Egypt and faced the brothers who betrayed him, he did not interpret his suffering as divine neglect. He declared, *"You intended to harm me, but God intended it for good"* (Genesis 50:20).

The manuscript had always been in God's hands.

In the New Testament, the resurrection stands as the ultimate confirmation that God completes what He begins. The cross looked like failure. The stone looked final. But Sunday revealed that what seemed like an ending was only transition.

Heaven always sees further than earth.

Heaven Sees the Completed Manuscript

When we read a novel, we move page by page, unaware of twists until they unfold. Yet the author has already finished the story before we begin reading.

Heaven sees your life that way.

In Revelation, Christ declares, *"I am the First and the Last."* The One who initiated your story already stands at its conclusion. He is not anxious about the outcome. He is not surprised by detours. He does not revise in panic.

What feels unresolved to you is already resolved in His wisdom.

Daniel Varghese once believed that the collapse of his business was the final chapter of his calling. Bankruptcy papers felt like punctuation marks at the end of a dream. But over time, through rebuilding and rediscovering dependence on God, he realized something profound: what he thought was the end was actually revision.

The collapse did not cancel his destiny. It clarified it.

Leah George, navigating grief after her mother's passing, once wondered if joy had permanently diminished. In the early months, sorrow colored everything. But gradually, compassion deepened. Sensitivity to others' pain expanded. Faith matured beyond surface gratitude.

The chapter that felt like loss became one of depth.

Heaven never lost sight of the completed manuscript.

You Are Not Abandoned in Process

One of the enemy's most persistent lies whispers loudly in the middle: *"God has left you."*

Left in the waiting.

Left in the confusion.

Left in the unanswered prayer.
But Scripture speaks differently.
When Israel wandered in the wilderness for forty years, it appeared directionless. Yet Deuteronomy 8 reveals that God was leading them, humbling them, teaching them dependence. The wilderness was not abandonment; it was preparation.
When Paul sat imprisoned in Rome, his mobility was restricted, but his influence multiplied. Letters written in chains would shape believers for centuries.
The middle is not evidence of neglect. It is evidence of development.
God does not desert what He designs. He does not discard what He calls. He does not initiate what He refuses to complete.
You are not stuck. You are being shaped.

You Are Being Written

Perhaps the most comforting truth of all is this: your life is not random ink scattered across blank pages. It is a narrative crafted by a faithful Author.
There are scenes you would have removed. Chapters you would have shortened. Twists you would have avoided. Yet the Author sees cohesion where you see confusion.
When Abraham walked toward Mount Moriah, he did not know provision was waiting. When Mary Magdalene wept outside the tomb, she did not realize resurrection was moments away. When Paul wrote from prison, he did not know his words would travel through centuries.
They were living in the middle.
And so are you.
Do not fear the unfinished chapter. Do not interpret delay as denial. Do not mistake silence for absence.

The Alpha who began your story is faithful. The Omega who completes it is sovereign. Between those eternal declarations, your life is unfolding with divine intention.

One day, what feels uncertain will make sense. What feels fragmented will reveal design. What feels delayed will display purpose.

Until then, trust the Author.

You are not abandoned in process.

You are being written.

About the Author
'GERARD ASSEY'

Gerard Assey is a Graduate in Economics, a PGD in Management (HRD) and holds a Doctorate in Leadership. Gerard holds several International Qualifications in Sales, Debt Collection, Training & Teaching, and is a 'Fellow' of the prestigious 'Institute of Sales & Marketing Management'-UK, a Certified NLP Practitioner, a 'Certified Trainer', an 'Accredited Management Teacher-Behavioral Sciences', a 'Certified Competency Facilitator', a 'Certified Management Consultant'- (the International credentials of a professional management consultant, awarded in accordance with global standards of the ICMCI); and a Certification from the University of Michigan in 'Successful Negotiation: Essential Strategies and Skills'

He is also a Member of the 'National Association of Sales Professionals' backed with several years experience in varied industries, both in India and Overseas. He also holds an 'Etiquette Consultant' Certification from the USA (by Sue Fox, Author of Best Seller: 'Business Etiquette for Dummies'. She has trained some of the top celebrities' world over). He was also a recipient of a scholarship for extensive training in Japan on 'Corporate Management for India'.

Gerard Assey is 'Founder & Chief Corporate Trainer' of the Group: **'Citius, Altius, Fortius Unlimited'**- an organization that **celebrated 20 years of Glorious Service** in 2021, focusing on 3 Core Competencies:

People. Performance. Profit; in functional areas of Sales & Marketing, HR & Organizational Development, covering Recruitment, Training & Consultancy!

Having managed organizations with large Sales Forces in India & Overseas, his specialization cover extensive areas of Sales Training (All levels - Presentation, Negotiation, Key/ Strategic Accounts Management & Managerial Skills for all sectors), Bid Proposal/ Capture Planning/ Management Trainings, Retail Sales, Customer Service & Customer Retention Programs, Training for Prevention & Collection of Debt, Self & Personal Development Programs (Time Management, Teamwork & Team Building, Business Etiquette & Personal Grooming, Leadership & Managerial Skills, People Management Skills, Train-the-Trainer etc), including preparation of Custom-designed Business Manuals for Internal (HR, Induction, and Sales etc) & External use (Instruction, User Manuals).

Gerard has successfully conducted over 6500 Trainings & Workshops (as of Feb '26) all across India, Middle East, Africa, Europe & S.E. Asia. Besides public programs conducted regularly, both in India & Overseas, he has some of the top names as clients whom he services from Single Owners to large Public & Government undertakings, covering all sectors, for their in-house needs.

His website: www.CollectionSkills.com is the only one in this part of the world to be featured in the 'Collections & Credit Risk Magazine-USA' under 'Who's Who in Training' and ranks TOP, along with other websites listed below on most search engines.

Gerard is author of 218 Books already (Feb 2026), all the books being available on all online platforms and outlets as E-books and Paperbacks

A few of our business related books:

1. Bite-sized Bits on Commonsense Management
2. Heart to Heart on Life's Principles'
3. How to become a Successful Manager
4. The Sales Professionals' Master Workbook of S.Y.S.T.E.M.S
5. The Professional Business Email Etiquette Handbook & Guide
6. The Professional Business Video-Conferencing Etiquette Handbook & Guide
7. Professional Presentation Skills
8. Exceptional Customer Service
9. Professional Tele-Marketing Skills
10. Professional Debt Collection Skills
11. The G.R.E.A.T. Sales & Service Workbook
12. Sales Training Advantage for Results (*The Ultimate Sales Training Manual to enable you stand out as a S.T.A.R.*)
13. CEO Daily Planner & Organizer
14. The Sales Professionals' Master Daily Planner
15. The Professional Debt Collector's Master Daily Planner
16. My Daily Planner & Organizer
17. MY EMERGENCY INFORMATION RECORD (Family Emergency & Peace of Mind Planner)
18. The Ultimate Therapist & Counselors Planner and Organizer
19. Building an Ethical Workplace
20. Managing Relationships at Work
21. Managing Business Meetings Effectively
22. Effective Delegation Skills
23. Goal Setting for Success
24. B2B Selling by Email
25. Professional Business Etiquette & Grooming
26. Dining Etiquette & Table Manners
27. Effective Networking Skills
28. Grooming, Etiquette & Manners for Teens, Young Adults & Future Leaders
29. Inter-Personal Skills
30. Get Ready, Get Hired!
31. Selling in a Recession
32. Effective Receivables Management in an Economic Downturn!
33. Real Estate & Property Sales Training
34. Credit Sales & Accounts Receivable Management

35. Selling Skills for Real Estate & Property Advisors
36. Take G.R.E.A.T. C.A.R.E!
37. Spa, Salon & Health Club Selling Skills
38. Selling Travel, Holiday & MICE Services
39. Selling Skills for Spa's, Salons & Health Clubs
40. Retailing in Salons & Spas
41. Selling Holiday, Vacation, Tours & Packages
42. The Power of Sales Referrals
43. Selling Luxury
44. Technical Selling Skills
45. Financial Advisors Sales Training
46. Dealing with Burnout at Work Monopolize Your Markets
47. Selling to Affluent Customers
48. Growing up with Grace
49. Financial Selling Skills
50. *The Effective Manager's Guide: Key Skills to Thrive*
51. From Aspiring to Inspiring: A Guide for New Managers on the Rise
52. The Power of Focus
53. Selling with Integrity: Sell Like Jesus The Perfect Role Model!
54. 31 Habits of Champions: Your 31-Day Journey to Greatness
55. Rejecting Grasshopper Talk: From Grasshopper to Giant-Killer-*Defeating Giants Daily!*
56. Navigate the AI-Powered Future of Bid & Proposals: Up-Skill to Stay Relevant with Alternative Career Paths & Opportunities
57. Hiring Sales Winners
58. Present with Impact
59. Success Unlocked: *Breaking Free from Habits that Hold You Back*
60. Complaints to Cheers, Feedback to Gold: Mastering Complaints Management
61. Thriving Together: *Cultivating Diversity, Equity, and Inclusion*
62. Coaching Skills for Sales Managers
63. Soaring to Success in Business & Leadership: Swifter, Higher, Stronger!
64. From Classroom to Podium: A Student's Guide to Powerful Public Speaking & Presentation Skills
65. Developing Self-Discipline
66. The CEO's 31-Day Power Plan: Unlocking Success through Essential Traits

67. Credibility Matters
68. A Winning Attitude
69. Bid & Proposal Management Using AI
70. Sales Forecasting: A Practical & Proven Guide to Strategic Sales Forecasting
71. Elevate & Energize: *50 Dynamic & Fun Activities for Peak Workplace Morale*
72. 'Sales SOS! Sales on Fire! *30 Days to Conquer Chaos & the Nightmares of Success!'*
73. Mastering Sales Managerial Skills: *Building High-Performing Teams & Driving Exceptional Results*
74. Eagle-Eyed Leadership: Unleashing the Power of 31 Lessons from Eagles
75. The Ultimate Employee Training Guide: *Training Today, Leading Tomorrow*
76. Being More Accountable at Work
77. Creating a Culture of Continuous Improvement
78. Effective Questioning & Listening Skills
79. The Power of Value Selling
80. The Growth Mindset
81. Mastering Professional Help Desk Skills
82. The Power to Lead with Empathy
83. Being Prepared: The Key to Unlocking Success
84. Youthful Spark-Youth Energizers, Activities and Games-Igniting the Fun in Youth
85. Ignite your Motivation for Success
86. Elevate Your Executive Presence: *Your Roadmap to Executive Excellence*
87. Smart Decisions: *Mastering Problem Solving with Strategic Solutions for Business Success*
88. Strategic Planning: *Developing and Implementing Strategic Plans to Achieve Long-Term Business Goals*
89. The Power of Stay Interviews
90. Developing G.R.I.T.
91. Adaptability
92. Diagnosis- *A Key Skill for Leadership*
93. The Burnout-Proof Salesperson: *The Master Guide to Preventing Stress & Burnout-* Strategies for Thriving in Sales
94. Learning from Failure: *Keys to Success*
95. Customer Success Management
96. Overcoming the Killers of Motivation
97. The C-Suite Code: *Mastering Skills for Executive Excellence'*

98. Dealing with Difficult Customers
99. Unlocking Your Potential: Mastering the Top 20 Life Skills for a Brighter Future
100. Nurturing Tomorrow's Leaders: *Essential Soft Skills Every Child Must Learn*
101. Lively & Fun Party Games for Seniors & Elders
102. Role Playing for Sales Champions: From Practice to Performance
103. Fun and Exciting Party Games for Kids
104. Case Studies for Sales
105. Role-Playing for Unbeatable Customer Service
106. Case Studies in Customer Service
107. Case Studies in Winning Negotiations
108. Case Studies in Management & Leadership
109. Case Studies in Human Resources & Talent Management
110. CEO Success Blueprint: The Essential Toolkit for CEOs and C-Level Executives
111. The Salesperson's Self-Coaching Guide: *Master Your Own Self-Coaching Plan for Success*
112. Overcoming Procrastination: *Your Ultimate Guide to Stop Delaying and Start Living Your Best Life*
113. When True Colors Are Exposed: *The Journey to Unmasking Humanity*
114. Life-Changing Habits for Teens: Teen Success Blueprint for a Bright Future
115. Workplace Stress-Free: *Proven Strategies to Thrive at Work and Beyond*
116. Objection Overruled: *The Ultimate Guide to Turning 'No' into 'Yes'*
117. Building Strong Teams: *A Comprehensive Guide to Team Building*
118. Ethical & Moral Leadership in Business: Eliminating Unethical Practices & Building a Culture of Trust & Integrity
119. Rising Strong: Building Positive: High Self-Esteem for a Fulfilling Life-*A Practical Guide for Students, Employees, Leaders & Entrepreneurs*
120 The Cheerful Mindset: Cultivating a Joyful Outlook Everyday
121. Leading Through Crisis: Case Studies on Crisis Management
122. Selling Beyond the Algorithms

From the Ministry side, Gerard graduated in the very first batch of Charis Bible College-India & had for over 9 years served as a Part-time Faculty at Charis Bible College-Chennai (Andrew Wommack Ministries-Colorado, USA).
He also holds a Diploma in Worship (a subject closest to his heart) from the JSOW and is also a graduate of the Advanced Mentorship Program (AMP) and the Circle Of Ministerial Engagement (C.O.M.E.) of Prophet Jerome Fernando and a Spiritual Son of the Esteemed Prophet.
An accomplished author of several Secular & Christian Books, Gerard has been on the board of a few international organizations and boasts of being the SON of the MOST HIGH GOD: An ordinary guy following an extraordinary GOD!

...And some of his most recent Christian Books being:

1. A Bouquet of Praises for My KING
2. Christian Jokes for the Serious Religious' Folks!
3. Jesus Healed You!
4. Praise24Ever! (also in Tamil version)
5. The 5G Network of GOD
6. Building Faith over F.E.A.R- FACE EVERYTHING AND RISE with JESUS
7. Hebrew and Greek Praise and Worship Words
8. Godly Mothers' and Grandmothers' Bible Story time for Kids!
9. Miracles of Jesus in Pictures
10. Raise your Praise all 365 Days
11. Thanking GOD with an Attitude of Gratitude
12. Meditating on the Attributes of GOD
13. Puppet Scripts
14. Alcohol Ruins, JESUS Reforms, Renews & Restores!
15. Habakkuk 2:2 Christian Daily Journal, Planner & Organizer
16. ABC of GOD's Word for Handwriting Practice
17. Daily Bible Verse Handwriting Practice (Building Godly Character & Faith through Cursive Handwriting Practice!)
18. Guiding Light: Fun & Faith-Building Bible Activities for Children
19. Rejecting Grasshopper Talk: From Grasshopper to Giant-Killer-*Defeating Giants Daily!*
20. Teen Titans of Faith: *Building Courage, Determination & Christ-like-Esteem*
21. I AM Empowered: *Unleashing Divine Power with Positive Declarations*

22. Be A Solution Provider-*From Passion to Purpose*: *A Biblical Guide to Being the Answer to the World!*
23. Miracles of JESUS
24. Parables of Jesus for a Meaningful Life!
25. A Grateful Heart: Importance of Sharing Testimonies of GOD's Grace
26. Melodies of Worship to JESUS: 31 Songs of Praise & Worship From My Heart to HIS!
27. I AM SO BLESSED!
28. My Daily Cup of Energizer
29. 31 Leadership Lessons *from* Jesus- *The Supreme Leader*
30. Peace Amidst Storms: A Biblical Guide to Conquering S.T.R.E.S.S.
31. Rise Above: 20 Biblical Eagle Lessons for Life's Triumphs
32. Godly Goal Setting: *The FAITHFUL Blueprint for a Purpose-Driven Life*
33. The Profound Attributes of our Mighty GOD: Understanding the 10S's of the Almighty
34. Worship Now, Worship Forever: *A Journey from Earthly Praise to Eternal Glory*
35. Unceasing Praise & Worship: *365 Days to Worship the King*
36. The ROAR Within: *Living with Purpose and Authority through the Power of the Holy Spirit*
37. From Potential to Purpose: Unlocking and Multiplying Your Talents & Gifts for Kingdom Impact
38. Songs from the Heart: *Worshipping GOD in Your Own Tune & Melody*
39. Awakening Praise & Worship: Hebrew & Greek Words to Raise Your Praise
40. Sing a NEW Song to the LORD Everyday: *Daily Devotions of Praise & Worship to Lift Your Heart & Glorify HIS Name*
41. *The* A.R.O.M.A. of True Worship: *Creating Worship That Delights God*
42. Becoming A Kingdom Champion: *Embracing God's Call for a Life of Purpose & Victory*
43. The Busy Businessman's Daily Devotional: 366 Crisp Truths to Start Your Day Strong
44. The Teacher's Heart: *Daily Devotions for Educators*
45. Anchored! *A 31-Day Devotional for Students Facing Life's Challenges*
46. Suddenly! Unlocking Unorthodox Breakthroughs through Unusual Worship
47. Overcoming Adversity: *Lessons from the Bible for Modern*

Challenges

48. LORD, Don't do it without me
49. Kingdom Leadership: *Biblical Principles for Modern Leaders*
50. Heartprints of God- *Growing God's Way:* Daily Devotions for Kids to Shine Bright
51. Send Judah First: Let your Praises Go up First to See the Mighty Move of GOD
52. DIVINE MOMENTS: *Recognizing, Embracing, Preparing, and Walking into Life-Changing Encounters with God*
53. Be a Builder in the Kingdom: *The C.E.M.E.N.T. Guide to Creating a Lasting Legacy*
54. Unshakable: *Pillars of Godly Womanhood* (Pillars of Faith That Changed History)
55. Lead Like a Shepherd: *14 Essential Traits for Pastoral Excellence*
56. The Worship Leader's Arsenal: *Powerful Exhortations to Ignite Thanksgiving, Praise & Worship*
57. Women of UnShakable Faith: *31-Day Devotional for Strength, Purpose & Influence*
58. Called to Teach: *A Complete 10-Week Training Guide for Impactful VBS Teachers*
59. Strumming for the KING: Cowboy Songs of Faith & Fire
60. The Ultimate Youth Camp Playbook: *50 Bible-Centered Indoor Games to Engage, Equip, and Empower Teens*
61. Glad in HIS Presence: *David's Revelation of GOD's Love & Mercy*
62. The Spirit Behind the Sound: *52 Devotionals for Worship Teams*
63. THE COWBOY'S COMPASS: *Riding the Trail of Faith with Grit & Grace*
64. Worship as My Weapon: *Living Victoriously through the Power of Praise*
65. A Worshipper Always Wins*: Living a Life of Victorious Worship*
66. Worship That Leads to the Throne: *Practical Strategies for Worship Leaders to Inspire Their Team & Usher People into God's Presence*
67. Worship as Warfare: *Conquering through the Sound of Surrender*
68. Watchmen on the Walls: *A 31-Day Devotional for Worship Teams*
69. KINGDOM BUSINESS: *52 Biblical Principles for GODLY*

Leadership & Wise Decisions

70. From Evening to Morning: *Rediscovering GOD's Sacred Hours*
71. Waves of Glory: *Worship through Dance, Flags, Staff & Sound*
72. WORSHIP TEAM BUILDER: *Guiding Your Team from Formation to Fruitfulness*
73. The Worship Leader's Master Training Manual
74. Skits for the King: Children's Plays for Every Church Occasion
75. Unbreakable: Building Strong Marriages and Families God's Way *(From Vows to Victory)*
76. Songs for my King: *A 31-Day Journey of Praise*
77. Building Powerful Children: *Raising a Generation That Will Shape the Future for God*
78. Character Before Chords: *The Heart of the True Worshipper*
79. 365 Days Before His Throne: A Worshipper's Daily Declarations
80. Broken to Built: *How GOD Restores Lives, Heals Hearts & Uses Broken People for HIS Glory*
81. Fear Did Not Come from God: *Discerning the Source, Dismantling the Stronghold & Walking in Power, Love & a Sound Mind*
82. THE GOD OF BEGINNINGS: *Positioning Your Life for What God Is About to Start*
83. HEALED ALREADY: IT IS FINISHED! Receiving What the Cross Has Completed!
84. A.D.D.E.D. Y.E.A.R.S. When God Overrules the Clock, the Diagnosis, and the Final Word
85. HALLELUJAH -The Sound That Heaven Understands *(Building a Life of Pure Praise)*
86. Worship in the Marketplace, Worship Beyond the Walls: *(Turning Work into Worship)*
87. ALPHA & OMEGA: *Living Secure Between the Beginning and the End*

Besides regularly contributing to business & trade journals, including international ones such as the 'Creative Training Techniques' and the 'Sales News' of the U.S.A, He is also a member of several prestigious bodies & trade associations, having participated in many Conferences & Workshops in India & Overseas.

Prior to his last assignment of leading & managing a large MNC as head, Gerard had a 3-year stint in the Middle East as a Consultant with a leading British Consultancy Firm.

As the past 'Official Country Representative' for the International Business Award- 'THE STEVIES'-(the business world's own Oscar) for about 4 years- he ensured a few Indian companies that qualify for the same every year!

Gerard can be contacted at:

Email: training@Sales-Training.in,training@CollectionSkills.com
Websites:

www.Sales-Training.in
www.EtiquetteWorks.in
www.CollectionSkills.com
www.RetailSalesTraining.in
www.SalesTrainingIndia.com
www.ManualPreparation.com
www.TrainingWithPuppets.com
www.FirstContactAcademy.com
www.SalesAndMarketingRecruiter.com

www.ingramcontent.com/pod-product-compliance
Ingram Content Group UK Ltd.
Pitfield, Milton Keynes, MK11 3LW, UK
UKHW021341190726
13845UKWH00027B/663